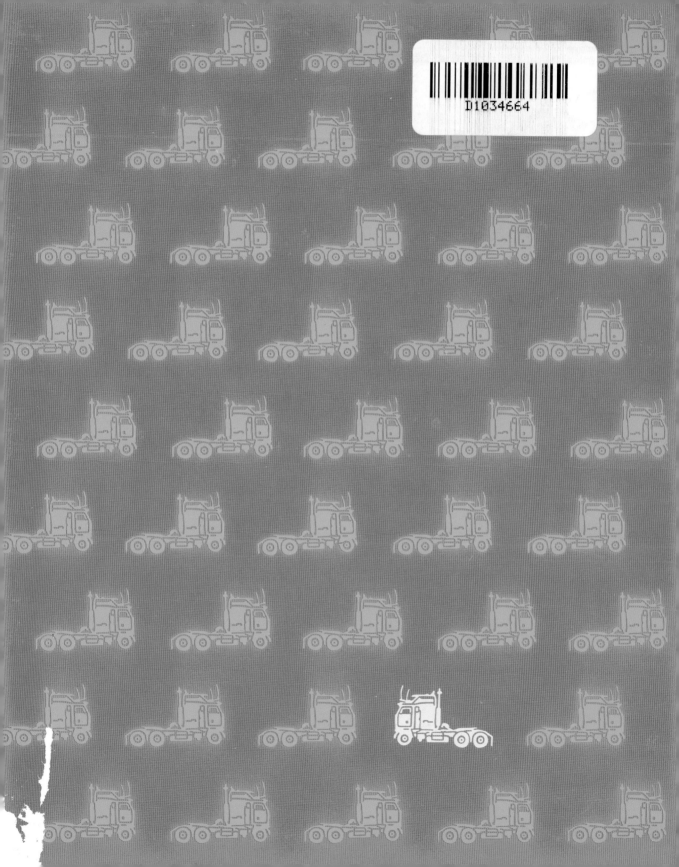

A DORLING KINDERSLEY BOOK
Conceived, edited, and designed by DK Direct Limited

Note to parents

What's Inside? Trucks is designed to help young children understand how different trucks work. It shows some surprises inside a container truck, how a garbage truck holds a whole neighborhood's trash, and all the equipment stored inside a fire engine. It is a book for you and your child to read and talk about together, and to enjoy.

Editor Hilary Hockman
Designers Juliette Norsworthy and Helen Spencer
Typographic Designer Nigel Coath
U.S. Editor Laaren Brown

Illustrators Richard Manning and Ed Stuart
Photographer Matthew Ward
Written by Alexandra Parsons
Consultants Ted Taylor and Jeff J. Middlebrook
Design Director Ed Day
Editorial Director Jonathan Reed

First published in Canada in 1992
by Grolier Limited,
14 Overlea Boulevard, Toronto, Ontario M4H 1P5
Telephone (416) 425-1924   Fax (416) 425-8858

Canadian Cataloguing in Publication Data
Parsons, Alexandra
Trucks
(What's Inside?)
ISBN 0-7172-2915-7

1. Trucks – Juvenile literature. I. Ward, Matthew. II. Manning, Richard, 1947-
III. Stuart, Ed. IV. Title. V. Series.
TL230.15.P37 1992   j629.224   C92-094341-1

First printed 1992. Printed and bound by L.E.G.O., Vicenza, Italy

WHAT'S INSIDE?

TRUCKS

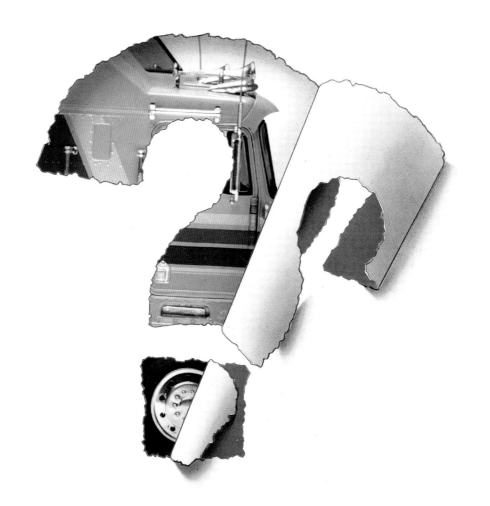

Grolier Limited
Canada

DRIVER'S CAB

The cab of a truck is designed to keep the driver comfortable and wide awake for safe driving. Cabs often have built-in beds so drivers can rest whenever they get tired. Many truck drivers will spend most of their working lives in cabs like this.

Trucks have diesel engines which use diesel fuel, not gasoline. Diesel engines drive big heavy vehicles like trucks, tractors, trains, and ships.

This deflector makes the passing air travel smoothly up and over the body of the truck.

Fumes from the engine come out through this pipe.

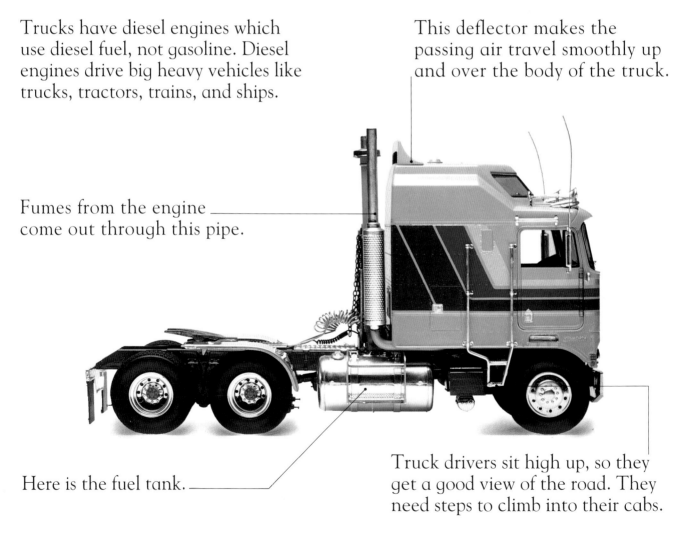

Here is the fuel tank.

Truck drivers sit high up, so they get a good view of the road. They need steps to climb into their cabs.

It can get lonely driving a truck. Some truck drivers keep in touch with each other using special radios called CBs.

Here's the driver's buddy. It's summer vacation, so young Juliette is spending some time on the road with her father!

The big, powerful engine is right here, between the driver and the passenger seat.

These bunks are for the driver and his friend. Cozy, isn't it? Drivers often have to stop in the middle of nowhere to rest.

There's even a little fridge built into the floor.

3

CONTAINER TRUCK

When goods are sent around the world on ships, they are packed into boxy containers that can easily be stacked and stored. Enormous cranes lift them in and out of ships. A container truck takes containers to and from the docks.

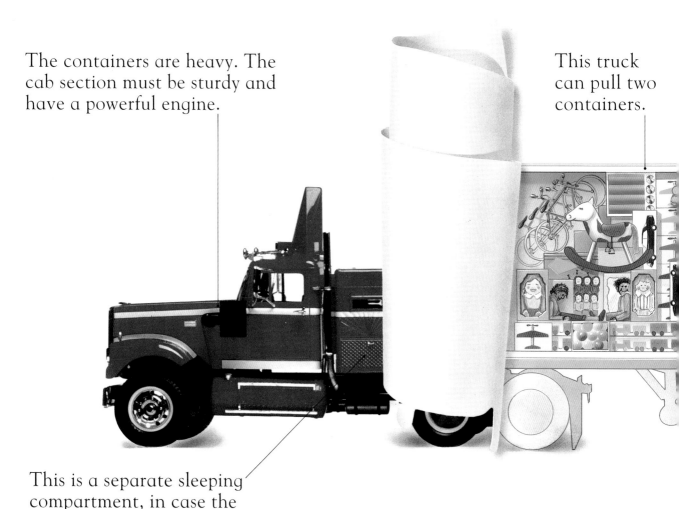

The containers are heavy. The cab section must be sturdy and have a powerful engine.

This truck can pull two containers.

This is a separate sleeping compartment, in case the driver gets tired.

Here's a fully loaded container ship. Containers are stacked on the deck as well as inside.

Containers are used again and again, so they have to be strong. They are made of steel.

When containers are full, they are fastened shut and sealed. They will not be opened until they arrive at their destination.

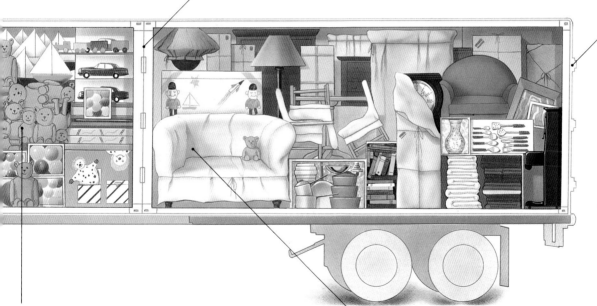

Here's a container from a toy factory. Maybe the things in these boxes will end up in a toy store near you.

This container is full of furniture and household things. Someone's family must be moving overseas.

AMBULANCE

Lights flashing, sirens wailing, ambulances rush sick and injured people to the hospital. When they arrive, doctors and nurses do their best to make the people better. The ambulance and its crew are part of the emergency team.

The flashing lights on the roof of the ambulance warn other traffic to get out of the way.

If you're in the ambulance, you can see out of these windows, but people can't see in.

Ambulance drivers are specially trained to drive fast but safely. They may have to weave in and out of the traffic, but they will keep the ambulance steady.

This patient will soon be at the hospital. She has a friend to keep her company.

People who have been in accidents must be kept warm. Ambulances always carry lots of warm blankets.

Only one side of an ambulance has windows. That leaves more room inside for the lifesaving equipment.

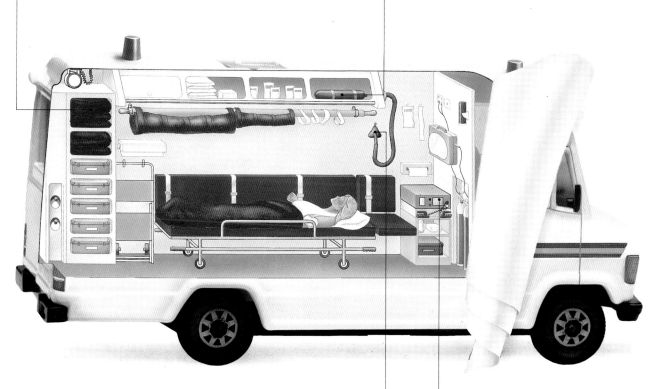

If someone needs help breathing, ambulance workers may give oxygen through this mask.

Here is the equipment used to get a person's heart going again if it has stopped.

TANKER

Tankers carry liquids such as gas and oil from the refineries, where fuels are made, to the garages and factories where they are needed. Tankers have special compartments inside to keep the contents clean and safe.

Every tanker has a special sign to say what it is carrying, in case there is an accident and the contents spill out onto the road. This is the sign for gasoline.

There is a ladder on the back...

...and a walkway along the top.

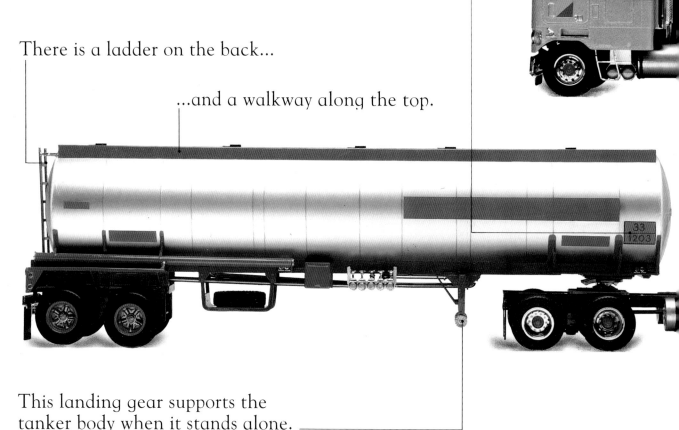

This landing gear supports the tanker body when it stands alone.

This tanker has five separate compartments. At the start of the trip, each one is filled through a manhole. There is one manhole for each compartment.

The inside of each compartment is lined with shiny aluminum. The insides are kept spotlessly clean because dirty fuel can clog engines.

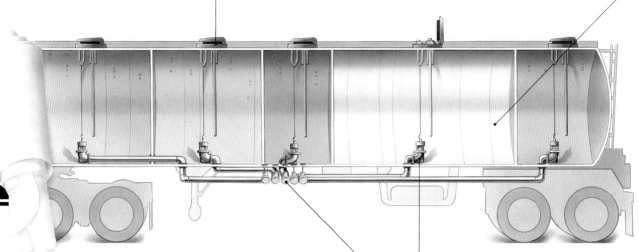

Each compartment has an outlet pipe. Gas is delivered to the garage through hoses attached to these outlets.

The compartments are not all the same size. Garages may need more of one kind of gas and less of another.

Not all tankers carry gasoline, of course. Some are specially made to carry milk, soda, or orange juice!

TRANSPORTER

Have you ever wondered how race cars get to racetracks? Well, now you know! This race-car transporter is a mobile garage and workshop as well as a high-tech computer center. It can carry up to five race cars.

At the front is the computer room. Here computers tell the technicians what the driver is doing. If the driver does something wrong, he might get a scolding over his headphones!

The radio keeps the driver in contact with his team in the transporter during a race. The top of the radio antenna is 40 feet above the ground.

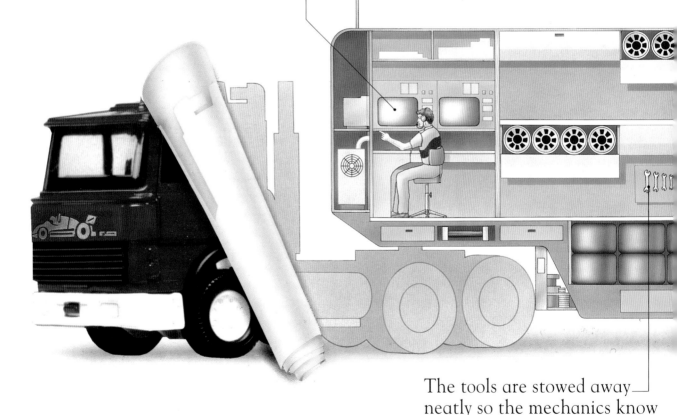

The tools are stowed away neatly so the mechanics know where everything is kept.

You will never see a race car on an ordinary road. They are allowed to drive only on racetracks.

Team and car both wear the team colors.

The back door acts as a lifting ramp to raise the cars up to the top level.

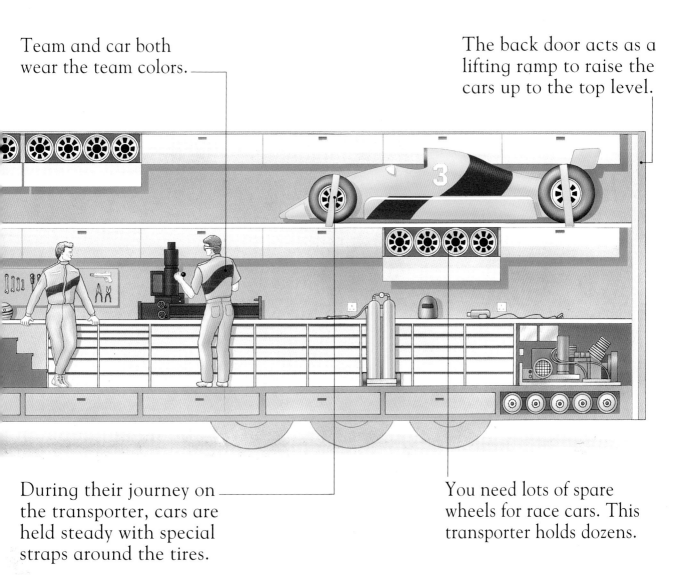

During their journey on the transporter, cars are held steady with special straps around the tires.

You need lots of spare wheels for race cars. This transporter holds dozens.

GARBAGE TRUCK

Once or twice a week, a garbage truck will come to your neighborhood to collect all the trash. Inside the truck, garbage is squeezed and squashed to make room for more. When the truck is full, everything goes to the dump.

The body of the truck is very strong so it won't bend while all the pushing and shoving goes on inside.

The driver and five or six sanitation workers travel in the cab.

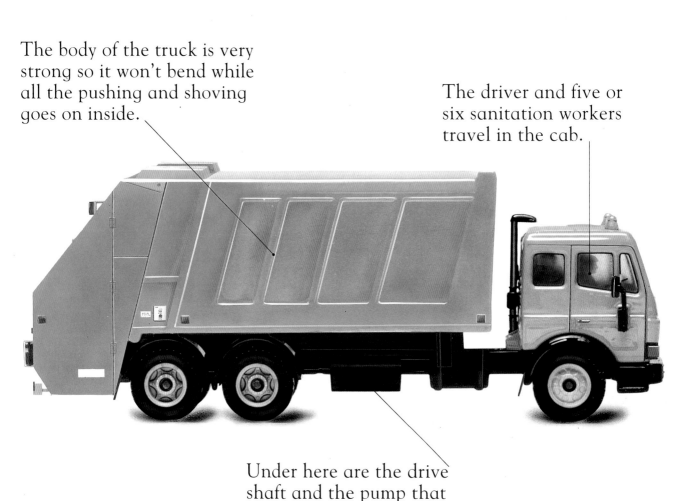

Under here are the drive shaft and the pump that make the compactor work.

What a bunch of junk! An average family throws out this much garbage every week.

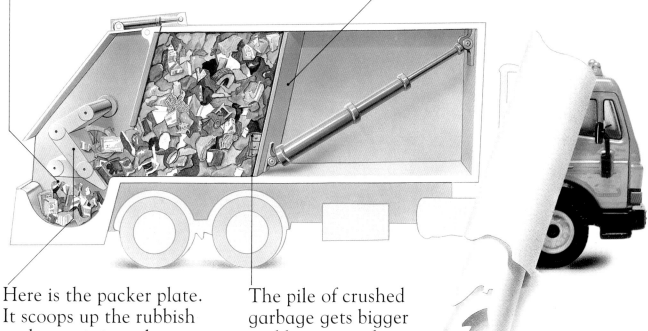

Trash goes into the loading hopper.

This is the ejector plate. When the garbage truck is full, the loading hopper lifts up and the ejector plate pushes the trash out.

Here is the packer plate. It scoops up the rubbish and rams it into the body of the truck.

The pile of crushed garbage gets bigger and bigger, and gradually pushes the ejector plate back.

HORSE TRAILER

When horses have to go to racetracks or shows, they travel in style in a horse trailer. These special trucks are like stables on wheels, with everything a horse needs for the journey.

There is room for two horses in this horse trailer.

Horses need fresh air just like we do. The air comes in through these openings.

Here is the loading ramp. Getting a horse in and out of a horse trailer requires kindness, understanding, and a tasty treat!

This horse trailer has no windows on the sides. If the horses could see traffic whizzing by, they might be frightened and try to break out.

They took all the jumps and didn't knock any of them down! The pony gets a red rosette pinned to its bridle, and the rider gets a little silver cup.

Horses can't move around inside a horse trailer to keep warm, so they wear woolly blankets.

Here is a snack for the journey. It is in a hay net.

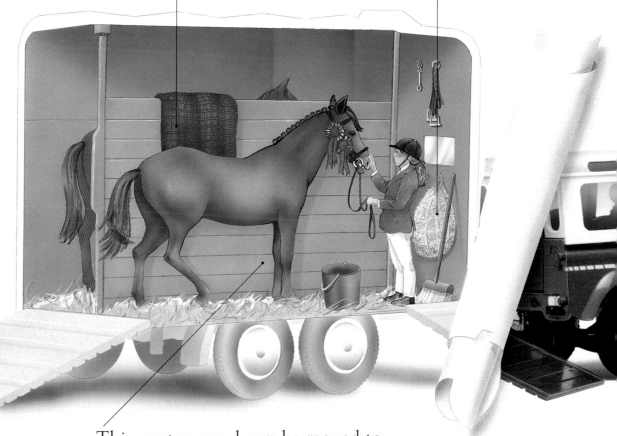

This center panel can be moved to make it easier to unload the horses.

FIRE ENGINE

A fire alarm rings out, and the fire fighters leap into action. They race through the streets in the fire engine, which is kept ready and waiting day and night. The job of fire fighters is to save lives and put out fires, and the fire engine helps them to do it.

Get out of the way! Flashing lights and loud horns warn other traffic to let the fire engine through.

Ladders are kept on the roof.

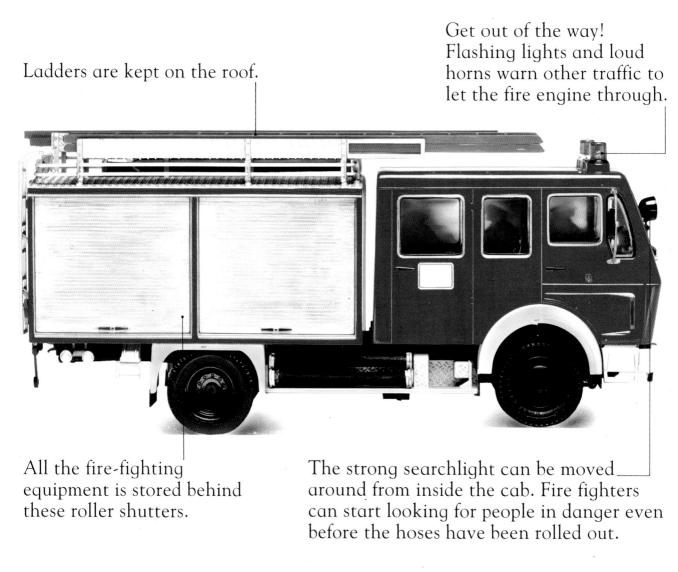

All the fire-fighting equipment is stored behind these roller shutters.

The strong searchlight can be moved around from inside the cab. Fire fighters can start looking for people in danger even before the hoses have been rolled out.

Sometimes going through the window is the only way to escape from a burning building.

There is a big water tank here...

... and a bottle of chemicals to make fire-fighting foam here.

Fire fighters need axes and saws to help them break down locked doors.

The hoses are stored here. Unwinding them is easy, but putting them away takes a long time.

The crew sits here while the fire engine races to a fire. They are still pulling on their boots as they speed along.